Frugal Living

Simple Tips and Tricks for a Better Life

Do-it-yourself Projects: How to Save Money by Fixing Things Yourself

Secondhand Shopping: How to Find Great Deals on Used Items

Working from Home: How to Save Money on Commuting and Work-Related Expenses

Freelancing: How to earn extra income from side hustles

Growing your own food: How to save money on groceries by growing your own produce

Retirement Planning: How to Save Money for the Future and Enjoy Retirement

Debt Reduction: How to Pay Off Debt and Improve Your Financial Situation

Insurance: How to find the right coverage and save money on premiums

Estate Planning: How to Protect Your Assets and Plan for the Future

Tax Planning: How to save money on taxes and take advantage of tax breaks

Online Shopping: How to Save Money by Shopping Online

Saving money on hobbies: How to enjoy your hobbies without spending too much

Money-saving apps: How to use technology to save money

Staying Committed to Frugality: How to Maintain Your Frugal Lifestyle Over Time

Conclusion

What is frugalism and why is it important?

Frugalism is a lifestyle that prioritizes spending less, saving more, and making wise financial decisions. It is about making the most of your resources, whether it's your time, money, or energy. Frugalism is not about depriving yourself of the things you enjoy or going without the necessities. Instead, it is about finding creative ways to save money and make your resources stretch further.

The reasons why frugalism is important can vary from person to person, but some common reasons include wanting to achieve financial independence, reducing debt, saving for retirement, or simply being able to live within your means. Frugal living can also help you simplify your life, minimize your impact on the environment, and reduce stress by reducing the pressure to keep up with the Joneses.

Frugality is a mindset that requires discipline, patience, and a willingness to change your habits. It requires you to be mindful of your spending, to make informed decisions, and to be willing to make sacrifices in the short-term for long-term gains. By embracing frugalism, you can take control of your finances, reduce your expenses, and improve your overall financial well-being.

Frugal living is not just about cutting costs, it's about making the most of what you have. It requires you to be creative, resourceful, and innovative. For example, instead of buying a new item, you might try repairing or repurposing something you already own. Or instead of eating out, you might try cooking a meal at home using ingredients you already have on hand. These small changes can add up over time and make a big impact on your finances.

In conclusion, frugalism is a way of life that empowers you to take control of your finances and achieve your financial goals. Whether you're looking to reduce debt, save for the future, or simply live within your means, frugalism can help you achieve your goals and improve your overall financial well-being.

The Psychology of Frugality: Understanding Your Motivations

Frugality is not just about cutting costs and saving money; it's also about understanding the underlying motivations and emotions that drive our spending habits. To truly embrace a frugal lifestyle, it's important to understand the psychological factors that influence our spending and develop strategies to overcome them.

One of the key psychological factors that influence our spending is the desire for instant gratification. We live in a fast-paced world where we want things now, and this desire can drive us to make impulsive purchases. To counteract this, it's important to take a step back and consider the long-term consequences of our spending decisions. A frugal lifestyle requires patience and a willingness to wait for things we want, rather than buying them on a whim.

Another psychological factor that influences our spending is the desire to fit in and be accepted by others. This can drive us to make purchases that we might not necessarily need or want, simply because we want to keep up with the Joneses. To overcome this, it's important to be confident in who you are and not be swayed by the opinions of others. Embrace the values and principles that are important to you, and don't be afraid to go against the norm.

Fear can also play a big role in our spending habits. We might be afraid of running out of money, or not having enough to cover our expenses in the future. This fear can drive us to overspend in an effort to feel secure. To overcome this, it's important to develop a strong financial plan, build an emergency fund, and understand the importance of living within your means.

Finally, our emotions can also play a big role in our spending habits. For example, we might make purchases when we're feeling happy or down to make ourselves feel better. To counteract this, it's important to recognize the role that emotions play in our spending and develop strategies to manage them. For example, you might take a walk, meditate, or engage in another activity that helps you manage your emotions in a healthy way.

In conclusion, the psychology of frugality is a complex and multi-faceted topic that requires a deep understanding of the motivations and emotions that drive our spending habits. By recognizing the psychological factors that influence our spending and developing strategies to overcome them, we can create a sustainable frugal lifestyle that allows us to take control of our finances and achieve our financial goals.

Budgeting Basics: How to Create and Stick to a Budget

Budgeting is a fundamental aspect of frugal living and one of the keys to taking control of your finances. A budget is a financial plan that helps you understand your income and expenses and provides a roadmap for reaching your financial goals. By creating a budget, you can gain clarity on your spending habits, identify areas where you can cut costs, and prioritize your spending in a way that aligns with your values and goals.

Creating a budget can seem overwhelming, but it's actually a simple process that anyone can do. The first step is to gather all of your financial information, including your income and expenses. You can do this by reviewing your bank statements, pay stubs, and credit card bills. This information will help you create an accurate picture of your finances.

Once you have all of your financial information, you can begin categorizing your expenses. Common categories include housing, transportation, food, entertainment, and personal care. You can use a spreadsheet or a budgeting app to help you keep track of your expenses. It's important to be honest and accurate when tracking your expenses, as this will help you make informed decisions about your spending.

After you've categorized your expenses, you can create a budget by subtracting your expenses from your income. This will give you a clear picture of your monthly surplus or deficit. If you have a surplus, you can use it to pay off debt, save for the future, or invest in your financial future.

If you have a deficit, you can look for areas where you can cut costs or increase your income.

Sticking to a budget can be a challenge, but there are a few strategies that can help. First, it's important to be realistic when creating your budget. If you set unrealistic goals, you'll be less likely to stick to them. It's also important to track your spending regularly and adjust your budget as needed. Finally, it's helpful to have a system in place that helps you stay accountable and on track. This might include using a budgeting app, working with a financial advisor, or simply talking to a trusted friend or family member about your budgeting goals.

Budgeting is an essential aspect of frugal living that can help you take control of your finances, reduce your expenses, and achieve your financial goals. By creating and sticking to a budget, you can create a sustainable financial plan that empowers you to live a more fulfilling and financially secure life.

Reducing Your Housing Costs: Tips for Finding Affordable Housing

Housing is often one of the largest expenses in a household budget, so reducing your housing costs can have a significant impact on your financial well-being. Whether you're a renter or a homeowner, there are a number of strategies you can use to reduce your housing costs and make your housing situation more affordable.

For renters, the first step in reducing your housing costs is to shop around for the best deal. This might mean looking for apartment buildings that offer discounts for long-term leases, or searching for rental properties in areas with lower rental costs. When shopping for rental properties, it's important to consider not just the monthly rent, but also the cost of utilities, parking, and other associated expenses.

Another strategy for reducing housing costs is to look for alternative housing options, such as shared housing or co-living arrangements. This can be an especially attractive option for single renters or those on a tight budget, as shared housing often allows you to split expenses like rent and utilities with other renters.

For homeowners, reducing housing costs can involve making changes to your home to make it more energy-efficient. This might mean installing insulation, upgrading your windows, or installing a programmable thermostat. These types of upgrades can reduce your monthly energy costs and improve the overall comfort of your home.

Another strategy for reducing housing costs is to downsize to a smaller home. This might mean selling your current home and moving to a smaller, more affordable home, or simply decluttering your current home to make it more manageable. Downsizing can be a great option for retirees, empty-nesters, or anyone looking to reduce their monthly expenses.

In conclusion, there are a number of strategies you can use to reduce your housing costs, whether you're a renter or a homeowner. By exploring your options and making changes to your housing situation, you can free up more of your monthly income for savings and other financial goals, and improve your overall financial security.

Frugal Food and Meal Planning: How to Save Money on Groceries

Food and grocery expenses can be a significant portion of a household budget, but there are a number of strategies that can help you reduce your food costs and save money on groceries. From meal planning to shopping at discount grocery stores, these tips can help you reduce your food expenses and improve your overall financial situation.

The first step in reducing your food expenses is to create a meal plan for the week. This will help you know exactly what you need to buy at the grocery store, and reduce the chances of overspending or impulse buying. When planning your meals, be sure to consider the dietary needs of your household, and look for recipes that use ingredients you already have on hand.

Another important strategy for saving money on groceries is to use coupons and discount codes. Many grocery stores offer coupons and discount codes through their websites and mobile apps, which you can use to save money on your weekly grocery purchases.

Shopping at discount grocery stores can also be an effective way to reduce your food expenses. Discount stores offer a limited selection of items at lower prices than traditional grocery stores. By shopping at these stores, you can save money on your groceries without sacrificing quality or variety.

In addition to shopping at discount stores, you can also reduce your food expenses by buying generic or store-brand products. These products are often just as good as their name-brand counterparts, but are priced significantly lower. When shopping for generic products, be sure to compare prices and ingredients to make sure you're getting a good deal.

Another strategy for reducing your food expenses is to buy in bulk. Buying items like rice, beans, and pasta in bulk can save you money in the long run, as long as you have the storage space to store the items. If you don't have enough storage space at home, you might consider joining a bulk food co-op in your community, where you can buy food in bulk with other members.

Finally, reducing food waste can also help you save money on groceries. By planning your meals, storing food properly, and using leftovers creatively, you can reduce the amount of food you throw away and save money on your grocery bill.

In conclusion, there are a number of strategies you can use to reduce your food expenses and save money on groceries. By meal planning, using coupons, shopping at discount stores, buying generic products, buying in bulk, and reducing food waste, you can reduce your food expenses and improve your overall financial situation.

Minimalism: How to Simplify Your Life and Save Money

Minimalism is a lifestyle choice that emphasizes living with less and prioritizing experiences over possessions. By simplifying your life and reducing clutter, minimalism can help you save money, reduce stress, and increase your overall sense of happiness and contentment.

One of the main benefits of minimalism is that it can help you save money. By owning fewer possessions, you have less to maintain and replace, which can reduce your overall expenses. Additionally, by avoiding impulse purchases and only buying what you truly need, you can reduce your spending and improve your financial situation.

Another benefit of minimalism is that it can help reduce stress and increase your sense of happiness and contentment. By owning fewer possessions, you have less to clean and maintain, which can free up your time and energy for more meaningful experiences. Additionally, by focusing on experiences rather than material possessions, you can shift your focus away from the pressures of consumer culture and towards what truly matters to you.

To get started with minimalism, it's important to begin by decluttering your home. This can involve sorting through your possessions and deciding what to keep, sell, or donate. When decluttering, it's important to be honest with yourself about what you actually use and need, and what is simply taking up space in your home.

Once you've decluttered your home, it's important to continue practicing minimalist principles in your daily life.

This can involve avoiding impulse purchases, only buying what you truly need, and choosing experiences over possessions. Additionally, it's important to maintain a minimalist mindset and continue to declutter your home as necessary, so that you can keep your life simple and free of clutter.

Another aspect of minimalism is being mindful of your consumption. This can involve reducing your waste and being more conscious of the products you buy and use. By reducing your waste, you can also reduce your environmental impact and save money by avoiding unnecessary purchases.

Minimalism can help you save money, reduce stress, and increase your overall sense of happiness and contentment. By decluttering your home, practicing minimalist principles in your daily life, and being mindful of your consumption, you can simplify your life and improve your financial situation.

Energy Efficiency: How to Reduce Your Utility Bills

Energy efficiency is the practice of reducing your energy consumption and reducing your impact on the environment. By making small changes in your home, you can reduce your energy usage, lower your utility bills, and improve your financial situation.

One of the most effective ways to reduce your energy usage is to upgrade your home's insulation. This can involve adding extra insulation in your attic, sealing air leaks around your windows and doors, and replacing old windows with more energy-efficient models.

Another way to reduce your energy usage is to upgrade your appliances and lighting. This can involve replacing old, inefficient appliances with Energy Star certified models, using LED light bulbs instead of traditional incandescent bulbs, and using programmable thermostats to control your heating and cooling system. By using energy-efficient appliances and lighting, you can reduce your energy usage and lower your utility bills.

In addition to upgrading your appliances and lighting, you can also reduce your energy usage by being mindful of your habits. This can involve turning off lights and electronics when you're not using them, setting your thermostat to an energy-saving temperature, and taking short showers instead of baths.

It's also important to be mindful of your energy usage when purchasing new appliances and electronics. When shopping for new appliances, look for Energy Star certified models, which are designed to use less energy and reduce your impact on the environment. Additionally, consider purchasing Energy Star certified electronics, such as televisions and computers, which are designed to be more energy-efficient.

Finally, you can reduce your energy usage by participating in energy conservation programs offered by your utility company. These programs can involve reducing your energy usage during peak periods, using energy-efficient appliances, and participating in energy audits to identify areas where you can improve your energy efficiency.

By making small changes in your home, being mindful of your habits, and participating in energy conservation programs, you can reduce your energy usage, lower your utility bills, and improve your financial situation. By adopting an energy-efficient lifestyle, you can help protect the environment and reduce your impact on the planet.

Shopping Smarter: Tips for Finding Deals and Avoiding Impulse Purchases

Shopping smarter is an important aspect of frugal living. One of the most effective ways to save money when shopping is to make a list of what you need and stick to it. Before you go shopping, take the time to plan out your purchases and make a list of the items you need. This will help you avoid impulse purchases and keep you focused on the items you actually need.

Another way to save money when shopping is to compare prices at different stores. This can involve checking online retailers, using price comparison websites, and visiting local stores to compare prices. By comparing prices, you can find the best deals and save money on your purchases.

In addition to comparing prices, you can also save money by using coupons and taking advantage of sales. This can involve clipping coupons from your local newspaper or subscribing to coupon websites, and checking your local stores for sales and clearance items. By using coupons and taking advantage of sales, you can save money on your purchases and improve your financial situation.

It's also important to be mindful of your habits when shopping. This can involve avoiding shopping when you're hungry, stressed, or tired, and avoiding shopping as a form of entertainment. By being mindful of your habits, you can reduce your impulse purchases.

Finally, you can save money by buying used items instead of new items. This can involve shopping at thrift stores, garage sales, and online marketplaces, such as eBay. By buying used items, you can save money on your purchases, reduce your impact on the environment, and support local communities.

In conclusion, by making a list, comparing prices, using coupons and taking advantage of sales, being mindful of your habits, and buying used items, you can save money, improve your financial situation, and reduce your impact on the environment. By shopping smarter, you can live a more frugal and sustainable life.

Investing in Your Future: How to Save Money for Retirement

Investing in your future is an important aspect of frugal living. By saving money for retirement, you can ensure a comfortable and secure future for yourself and your loved ones.

One of the most effective ways to save money for retirement is to start early. The earlier you start saving, the more time your money has to grow through compound interest. This means that the longer you save, the more money you'll have in retirement, even if you save a smaller amount each month.

Another way to save money for retirement is to take advantage of retirement savings accounts. These accounts are designed specifically for retirement savings and often offer tax benefits and employer matching contributions, which can help you save more money and grow your retirement savings more quickly.

In addition to retirement savings accounts, you can also save money for retirement by investing in stocks, bonds, and mutual funds. By investing in a diversified portfolio, you can reduce your risk and potentially earn a higher return on your investment. However, it's important to be mindful of your investment choices and seek the advice of a financial advisor if necessary.

Another way to save money for retirement is to live below your means. By reducing your expenses and avoiding debt, you can free up more money each month to save for your future. This can involve cutting back on unnecessary expenses, such as eating out and entertainment, and prioritizing your spending on essential expenses, such as housing, food, and transportation.

Finally, you can save money for retirement by increasing your income. This can involve taking on a part-time job, starting a side business, or asking for a raise at your current job. By increasing your income, you can save more money and grow your retirement savings more quickly.

In conclusion, by starting early, taking advantage of retirement savings accounts, investing in stocks, bonds, and mutual funds, living below your means, and increasing your income, you can save money for your future and ensure a comfortable and secure retirement.

Frugal Transportation: How to Save Money on Car Expenses and Alternative Transportation Options

Transportation is a significant expense for many people, but it doesn't have to be. By adopting a frugal mindset, you can save money on your transportation expenses and potentially eliminate this cost altogether.

One of the most effective ways to save money on car expenses is to maintain your vehicle properly. Regular maintenance, such as oil changes and tire rotations, can extend the life of your vehicle and reduce the need for expensive repairs. You can also save money on gas by driving efficiently, such as accelerating and braking smoothly and avoiding high-speed driving.

Another way to save money on car expenses is to consider alternative transportation options, such as public transportation, carpooling, and biking. By using alternative transportation, you can reduce the amount of time you spend driving and the amount of money you spend on gas, maintenance, and insurance.

In addition to alternative transportation, you can also save money on car expenses by purchasing a fuel-efficient vehicle. Hybrid and electric vehicles can significantly reduce your fuel costs and help you save money in the long run.

If you do need a car, consider purchasing a used vehicle rather than a new one. Used vehicles are often much less expensive than new vehicles and can still provide reliable transportation.

Finally, you can save money on car expenses by being mindful of your driving habits. This can include reducing the amount of time you spend driving and avoiding unnecessary trips. You can also reduce your driving expenses by carpooling, which can also help reduce your carbon footprint.

In conclusion, by maintaining your vehicle properly, considering alternative transportation options, purchasing a fuel-efficient vehicle, purchasing a used vehicle, and being mindful of your driving habits, you can save money on your transportation expenses and potentially eliminate this cost altogether.

Health and Wellness on a Budget: How to Stay Healthy Without Breaking the Bank

Maintaining good health is important, but it can also be expensive. By adopting a frugal mindset, you can stay healthy without breaking the bank.

One of the best ways to maintain your health is to eat a balanced diet that includes plenty of fruits, vegetables, whole grains, and lean proteins. You can save money on groceries by purchasing in-season produce, shopping at discount grocery stores, and meal planning. Meal planning can also help you reduce food waste and avoid impulse purchases.

Another way to stay healthy on a budget is to stay active. Physical activity is important for maintaining good health, and there are many low-cost or free ways to stay active, such as walking, hiking, and biking. You can also join a community sports team or participate in group fitness classes for a low cost.

In addition to physical activity, it's important to get enough sleep and manage stress. You can improve your sleep by establishing a consistent sleep schedule and creating a relaxing sleep environment. You can manage stress by practicing relaxation techniques, such as deep breathing and meditation, and engaging in activities that you enjoy.

You can save money on prescription medications by comparing prices at different pharmacies and asking your doctor if there are generic alternatives to your medications.

Finally, it's important to have health insurance. If you're not covered by an employer-sponsored health plan, consider purchasing a low-cost health insurance plan through the health insurance marketplace.

In conclusion, by eating a balanced diet, staying active, getting enough sleep and managing stress, considering alternative options for medications, and having health insurance, you can stay healthy without breaking the bank. By being frugal with your health and wellness, you can live a healthier and more affordable life.

Money-Saving Tips for Families: How to Raise Children Frugally

Raising a family can be expensive, but it doesn't have to be. By adopting a frugal mindset, you can provide your children with the best possible life while saving money in the process.

One of the best ways to save money as a family is to find low-cost or free activities to do together. This can include visiting parks and museums, participating in community events, and going on nature hikes. You can also save money on entertainment by subscribing to streaming services instead of cable TV, borrowing books and movies from the library, and creating your own fun at home with arts and crafts supplies.

When it comes to purchasing items for your children, consider purchasing used items or hand-me-downs instead of new items. This can include clothing, toys, and baby gear. You can also save money on school supplies by shopping sales and purchasing generic items.

Another way to save money as a family is to prioritize healthy eating habits. Cook meals at home instead of eating out, and pack your own lunches for work and school. You can also save money on snacks by purchasing in bulk and making your own healthy snacks, such as fruit and nut bars, at home.

It's also important to teach your children about the importance of saving money. Encourage them to save their allowance and teach them how to budget their money. You can also teach them about the importance of giving back by volunteering and donating to charity.

In conclusion, by finding low-cost or free activities to do together, purchasing used items, prioritizing healthy eating habits, and teaching your children about the importance of saving money, you can raise your children frugally and provide them with the best possible life. By being frugal as a family, you can build a strong financial foundation for the future.

Building an Emergency Fund: Why It's Important and How to Get Started

An emergency fund is a crucial aspect of personal finance. It acts as a safety net in case of unexpected events such as job loss, medical expenses, or home repairs. Without an emergency fund, you may end up going into debt or dipping into your savings, which can have long-term financial consequences.

The first step in building an emergency fund is to determine your emergency fund goal. A general guideline is to have three to six months of living expenses saved in case of a financial emergency. To calculate your living expenses, consider all of your monthly expenses, including housing, food, transportation, insurance, and other necessities.

Once you have determined your emergency fund goal, it's time to start saving. One of the best ways to save for an emergency fund is to automate your savings. You can set up a direct deposit from your paycheck into a separate savings account specifically for your emergency fund. This way, you can save without having to think about it.

Another way to build your emergency fund is to look for ways to reduce your monthly expenses. This can include cutting back on discretionary spending, such as dining out, entertainment, and shopping, and finding ways to reduce your monthly bills, such as negotiating your cable or internet bill.

You can also consider increasing your income through side hustles or asking for a raise at work. Any extra money you earn can be put directly into your emergency fund.

Building an emergency fund is crucial for financial stability. By determining your emergency fund goal, automating your savings, reducing your monthly expenses, and increasing your income, you can build a strong emergency fund to protect yourself and your family in case of financial emergencies. Don't wait until it's too late to start building your emergency fund - start today!

Frugal Travel: How to Take Vacations Without Going into Debt

Travel is a great way to relax, experience new cultures, and create memories that last a lifetime. However, it can also be expensive, and it's easy to end up spending more money than you planned. If you want to take vacations without going into debt, it's important to be mindful of your spending and adopt a frugal approach to travel.

One of the most important things you can do to save money on travel is to plan ahead. This means researching your destination, finding deals on flights and accommodations, and setting a budget for your trip. It's also a good idea to compare prices for different travel dates to find the best deals.

Another way to save money on travel is to look for alternative accommodations. Rather than staying in a hotel, consider staying in a vacation rental, hostel, or camping site. This can save you money on accommodations and provide you with a unique and immersive travel experience.

When it comes to meals, one of the best ways to save money is to cook your own food. This can be done by staying in a rental with a kitchen or by purchasing food from local markets and cooking it yourself. Eating at local restaurants can also be a fun and budget-friendly way to experience local cuisine.

It's important to be mindful of transportation costs. This can include the cost of getting to and from your destination, as well as transportation while you're there. Consider taking public transportation, walking, or biking, instead of renting a car. If you do need to rent a car, compare prices and consider car-sharing options.

Another way to save money on travel is to be mindful of your entertainment expenses. Look for free or low-cost activities, such as visiting museums or hiking in local parks. This can help you enjoy your trip without breaking the bank.

Finally, it's important to have an emergency fund for travel. This can help you cover unexpected expenses and ensure that your trip doesn't put you into debt.

Frugal travel is all about being mindful of your spending and finding ways to save money while still enjoying your trip. With a little bit of planning and preparation, you can take amazing vacations without going into debt.

Do-it-yourself Projects: How to Save Money by Fixing Things Yourself

DIY projects can be a great way to save money while also learning new skills and improving your home or personal items. Whether you're fixing a leaky faucet, repairing a piece of furniture, or building a bookshelf, taking on a DIY project can be a fun and budget-friendly activity. In this chapter, we'll cover tips for successfully completing DIY projects and how to make the most of your budget.

Getting Started:

- Determine the scope of the project: Before starting any project, it's important to understand what you're capable of doing and what tools and materials you'll need.
- Research and gather information: Look for tutorials or instructional videos online or consult a how-to book.
- Plan your budget: Determine the total cost of the project, including the cost of any necessary tools and materials.
- Gather tools and materials: Consider buying second-hand items or using what you already have instead of buying everything new.

Working on the Project:

- Work with a partner: Having a friend or family member work with you on the project can be helpful, both in terms of getting the job done more quickly and dividing the cost of tools and materials.

- Take your time: Rushing through a project can lead to mistakes and mistakes can be costly.
- Follow safety precautions: Make sure to wear protective gear and follow all safety measures to avoid injury.

Saving Money:

- Use coupons and discounts: Check for sales, coupons, and discounts at home improvement stores or online.
- Buy in bulk: If you're planning on taking on multiple projects, buying in bulk can save you money in the long run.
- Reuse materials: Try to reuse materials or items you already have before buying new ones.
- Compare prices: Take the time to compare prices of tools and materials at different stores to get the best deal.

Taking on DIY projects can be a great way to save money and improve your home or personal items. By following these tips, you can ensure that your projects are successful and budget-friendly. Whether you're fixing a broken item, building a new one, or just looking for a fun and cost-effective hobby, DIY projects can be a great option for anyone looking to live a more frugal lifestyle.

Secondhand Shopping: How to Find Great Deals on Used Items

Secondhand shopping is a great way to save money while still getting the things you need. Whether you are looking for clothing, furniture, electronics, or other items, there are many places to find gently used items at a fraction of the cost of buying new.

One of the most popular places to find secondhand items is at thrift stores. Thrift stores often receive donations from individuals, so the selection can be hit or miss, but you can often find great deals on items that are in excellent condition. Look for thrift stores in your area and make a habit of stopping in regularly to see what's available.

Another great place to find secondhand items is online. Websites like Craigslist and Facebook Marketplace allow you to search for items in your area and negotiate prices with the seller directly. These websites also have buyer protection policies, so you can feel confident that you are making a safe purchase.

Garage sales and estate sales are also great places to find secondhand items. Keep an eye on local listings and be prepared to get up early on weekends to beat the crowds.

When shopping for secondhand items, it's important to inspect items carefully before making a purchase. Look for signs of wear and tear, and ask the seller about the item's history and any known problems.

By incorporating secondhand shopping into your life, you can save money on the things you need while reducing your impact on the environment. With a little patience and creativity, you can find great deals on gently used items and create a more frugal and sustainable lifestyle.

Working from Home: How to Save Money on Commuting and Work-Related Expenses

Working from home has become increasingly common in recent years, and it offers many advantages, including the opportunity to save money on commuting and work-related expenses. By eliminating the need to travel to and from the office, you can save money on gas, public transportation, parking, and other commuting-related expenses.

In addition to saving money on commuting, working from home can also help you save money on work-related expenses. For example, you can save money on lunch by preparing your own meals, and you may also be able to save money on clothing by not having to wear business attire every day.

To maximize your savings while working from home, it's important to have a dedicated workspace that is separate from your living space. This will help you stay focused and productive, and it will also allow you to claim a home office deduction on your taxes, which can further reduce your tax liability.

When working from home, it's also important to be mindful of your energy usage. By turning off lights and electronics when not in use, you can reduce your energy bill and help the environment.

In addition to saving money, working from home can also offer more flexibility and control over your schedule. With the ability to work from anywhere with an internet connection, you can spend more time with family and friends, travel more, and enjoy a better work-life balance.

By embracing the benefits of working from home, you can achieve a more frugal and sustainable lifestyle. With a little planning and effort, you can save money on commuting and work-related expenses while enjoying the freedom and flexibility of working from home.

Freelancing: How to earn extra income from side hustles

Freelancing is a popular way for individuals to supplement their income and create a flexible work schedule. With the rise of the gig economy, it has never been easier to turn your skills and passions into a profitable side hustle. Whether you're an artist, writer, developer, or marketer, there are countless opportunities to offer your services as a freelancer.

Here are some tips for starting and growing a successful freelancing business:

1. Identify your niche: Think about what skills you have that could be in demand and research the job market to see what types of freelance work are available.
2. Build your portfolio: Create a portfolio that showcases your work and highlights your expertise. This will be crucial when reaching out to potential clients and bidding on projects.
3. Network: Join online communities, attend events, and connect with other freelancers to build your network and find new opportunities.
4. Set your rates: Research market rates for your niche and determine a price that accurately reflects your experience and skill level. Be confident in your pricing and be willing to negotiate when necessary.
5. Market yourself: Promote your services on social media, your personal website, and other platforms. Consider reaching out to potential clients directly and offering your services.

6. Manage your finances: Make sure to keep track of your income and expenses, set aside money for taxes, and consider investing in tools that can help you manage your business efficiently.
7. Stay organized: Keep track of deadlines, invoices, and project details so you can stay on top of your work and deliver quality results.

By following these tips, you can turn your freelance business into a successful and profitable venture. Whether you're looking to supplement your income or pursue a full-time career as a freelancer, it's never too late to start.

Growing your own food: How to save money on groceries by growing your own produce

Growing your own food is a great way to save money on groceries and eat healthier. By growing your own fruits and vegetables, you have control over the quality of the food you eat, and you can also reduce your carbon footprint by reducing the distance your food has to travel. There are many different ways to start growing your own food, whether you have a large backyard or just a small balcony.

1. Choose the right location: Make sure the area you choose has access to sunlight and is protected from wind and other harsh weather conditions. Consider factors such as soil type, water availability, and how much space you have available.
2. Choose the right plants: Choose plants that are well-suited to your growing conditions and climate. Consider the amount of space, sun exposure, and soil type when selecting plants. Also, choose plants that you and your family like to eat, this will make it easier to use the produce you grow.
3. Start small: If you're new to gardening, start with a few easy-to-grow plants like herbs, tomatoes, or lettuce. As you gain experience, you can add more plants to your garden.
4. Use containers: If you don't have much space or soil, consider using containers. Containers can be made of different materials, such as plastic, clay, or wood, and can be placed on balconies, patios, or windowsills.
5. Use organic methods: Avoid using chemicals and pesticides in your garden, and instead use organic

methods to control pests and diseases. This will make your food safer to eat, and also helps the environment.

6. Plan ahead: Make a plan for how you will use the produce you grow, so you can ensure that you're planting the right amount of each plant. Plan to preserve some of your produce for use during the winter months.

By growing your own food, you can save money on groceries, eat healthier, and reduce your carbon footprint. It's also a great way to spend time outside, get some exercise, and connect with nature. Whether you have a large backyard or just a small balcony, there is a way for you to start growing your own food.

Retirement Planning: How to Save Money for the Future and Enjoy Retirement

Retirement planning is a crucial aspect of financial planning that helps individuals ensure a comfortable and secure retirement. The purpose of this chapter is to help you understand the importance of retirement planning and how to save money for the future so that you can enjoy your retirement years.

Why is retirement planning important?

Retirement planning is important because it helps individuals prepare for the financial realities of retirement. The cost of living increases over time, and individuals need to have enough savings to maintain their standard of living in retirement.

How to save money for retirement?

1. Start early: The earlier you start saving for retirement, the more time your savings have to grow. The power of compounding interest means that your savings can grow exponentially over time, so starting early can have a significant impact on your retirement savings.
2. Create a budget: Create a budget that includes saving for retirement. Determine how much you can afford to save each month and make sure to stick to your budget.
3. Contribute to a retirement plan: Consider contributing to a retirement plan. Many employers offer matching contributions, which means you can

save more for retirement by contributing to your plan.

4. Invest wisely: Invest your retirement savings in a diversified portfolio of low-cost mutual funds or index funds. This can help you achieve higher returns and minimize your risk.

5. Consider other savings vehicles: Consider other savings vehicles, such as annuities or life insurance policies, to help you save for retirement.

6. Live below your means: To save more for retirement, you need to live below your means. This means spending less than you earn and avoiding debt as much as possible.

7. Plan for long-term care: Long-term care costs can be significant in retirement, so it's important to plan for them. Consider purchasing long-term care insurance or saving for long-term care in a special account.

Enjoying retirement

Retirement can be an exciting time, but it can also be stressful if you don't have enough savings to support yourself. By saving money for the future and planning for retirement, you can ensure that you have the financial security you need to enjoy your retirement years. Consider what you want to do in retirement, such as travel, spend time with family, or pursue hobbies, and make sure you have enough savings to support those activities.

In conclusion, retirement planning is a critical aspect of financial planning. By starting early, creating a budget, contributing to a retirement plan, investing wisely, and living below your means, you can save money for the future and enjoy a comfortable and secure retirement.

Debt Reduction: How to Pay Off Debt and Improve Your Financial Situation

Debt can be a heavy burden and impact your overall financial stability. Whether it's from credit cards, student loans, or personal loans, the goal of debt reduction is to pay it off as quickly as possible while minimizing interest costs.

Here are some steps to help you reduce your debt:

1. Assess Your Debt: Make a list of all your debts, including the creditor, interest rate, and minimum payment due. This will give you a clear picture of your financial situation and help you prioritize which debts to pay off first.
2. Create a Budget: Creating a budget is a crucial step in reducing debt. This will help you allocate funds to pay off your debts while still paying for necessary expenses.
3. Prioritize Your Debts: Pay off high-interest debt first, as it will cost you more in the long run. Consider using the debt snowball or debt avalanche method to prioritize your debt repayment.
4. Increase Your Income: Look for ways to increase your income, such as freelancing, side hustles, or asking for a raise. The extra income can be used to pay off debt faster.
5. Cut Expenses: Reducing expenses is another way to free up money to pay off debt. Look for ways to save money in your budget, such as cutting back on eating out or reducing your grocery bill.
6. Make Extra Payments: Make extra payments to pay off debt faster and save on interest costs.

7. Avoid Accruing More Debt: Once you start paying off debt, it's important to avoid accruing more debt. Avoid using credit cards and taking out loans unless it's necessary.

Debt reduction requires discipline and persistence, but the end result is worth it. By paying off debt, you will improve your financial situation and have peace of mind knowing that you're debt-free.

Insurance: How to find the right coverage and save money on premiums

Insurance is a crucial part of personal finance and protecting your assets, but it can also be one of the largest expenses in your budget. However, by understanding the different types of insurance, comparing policies, and shopping around, you can find the right coverage and save money on your premiums.

The first step to finding the right insurance coverage is to understand your needs. This may include health insurance, life insurance, auto insurance, homeowners or renters insurance, and liability insurance. By taking an inventory of your assets, liabilities, and future plans, you can determine which types of insurance you need and how much coverage you should have.

Once you have a clear understanding of your insurance needs, it's time to start comparing policies. Make sure to consider factors such as the coverage amounts, deductibles, and the reputation of the insurance company. It's also important to read the fine print and understand the exclusions, limitations, and the process for filing claims.

One of the best ways to save money on insurance premiums is to shop around. Get quotes from multiple insurance companies and compare their offerings. Don't be afraid to negotiate, as insurance companies often have room to lower their premiums to win your business.

Another way to save money on insurance is to bundle your policies. Many insurance companies offer discounts for customers who have multiple policies with them. For example, if you have both your auto and homeowners insurance with the same company, you may be eligible for a discount.

Finally, it's important to regularly review your insurance coverage to ensure it continues to meet your needs. Life events, such as getting married, having children, or buying a new home, can all impact your insurance needs, and it's important to make sure your coverage is updated to reflect these changes.

By following these tips, you can find the right insurance coverage and save money on your premiums. Protecting your assets and securing your future is essential, and with a little effort and research, you can do so while keeping your budget in check.

Estate Planning: How to Protect Your Assets and Plan for the Future

Estate planning is a critical component of a comprehensive financial plan. It involves organizing your assets and liabilities, making decisions about your future, and making arrangements for the distribution of your property after death. This chapter will help you understand the importance of estate planning and provide tips on how to protect your assets and plan for the future.

Why is estate planning important?

Estate planning is important for several reasons. It helps ensure that your wishes are followed, your assets are protected, and your loved ones are taken care of after your death.

What should be included in an estate plan?

An estate plan should include a will, trust, power of attorney, and advance health care directive. A will is a legal document that outlines how you want your property to be distributed after your death. A trust is a legal arrangement that allows you to hold and manage property for the benefit of someone else. A power of attorney gives someone else the authority to act on your behalf if you become incapacitated. An advance health care directive outlines your wishes regarding medical treatment if you become unable to make decisions for yourself.

How can you protect your assets?

There are several ways to protect your assets, including creating a living trust, purchasing insurance, and gifting property. A living trust allows you to transfer ownership of your property to a trustee while you are still alive. This can help reduce the tax burden on your estate and minimize the expenses associated with probate court proceedings. Insurance can provide financial protection for your loved ones in the event of your death. Gifting property can help reduce the size of your estate, making it easier to manage and reducing the tax burden on your estate.

In conclusion, estate planning is an important component of a comprehensive financial plan. It helps ensure that your wishes are followed, your assets are protected, and your loved ones are taken care of after your death. By including a will, trust, power of attorney, and advance health care directive in your estate plan, you can take control of your financial future and protect your assets.

Tax Planning: How to save money on taxes and take advantage of tax breaks

One of the key aspects of frugal living is maximizing your income and minimizing your expenses. This includes taking advantage of all the tax breaks and deductions you're eligible for. By understanding the tax code and planning your finances accordingly, you can significantly reduce your tax bill and keep more of your hard-earned money.

Here are some tips for effective tax planning:

1. Keep accurate records: To claim all the deductions and credits you're entitled to, it's essential to keep accurate records of your income and expenses. This includes receipts, bills, and bank statements.
2. Understand the different types of taxes: There are several types of taxes, including income tax, sales tax, property tax, and others. Understanding the different types of taxes will help you identify the deductions and credits that apply to you.
3. Take advantage of deductions: There are many deductions available, including those for mortgage interest, charitable donations, and medical expenses. By taking advantage of these deductions, you can significantly reduce your taxable income.
4. Consider tax credits: Tax credits are even more valuable than deductions because they reduce your tax bill dollar for dollar. For example, the Earned Income Tax Credit provides a significant tax credit to low-income taxpayers.
5. Plan for retirement: Retirement accounts offer tax benefits, including deductions for contributions and

tax-free growth of your investments. By contributing to these accounts, you can reduce your taxable income and prepare for a secure financial future.

6. Seek professional advice: Tax laws are complex and change frequently. By seeking the advice of a tax professional, you can ensure that you're taking advantage of all the deductions and credits available to you.

By following these tips, you can effectively manage your taxes and keep more of your hard-earned money. Remember, tax planning is an ongoing process that requires constant attention to detail and a thorough understanding of the tax code.

Online Shopping: How to Save Money by Shopping Online

Online shopping has become an increasingly popular way to purchase goods and services, providing consumers with convenience and a wide selection of products at their fingertips. Not only is it easier to compare prices and find discounts, but shopping online also provides an opportunity to save money. In this chapter, we'll explore the best ways to save money while shopping online.

1. Use Coupon Codes: One of the easiest ways to save money while shopping online is to use coupon codes. Many online retailers offer special discounts for customers who use a promo code during checkout. You can find these codes by doing a quick search on Google or on the retailer's website. Some retailers also offer email or mobile notifications for special sales and discounts.

2. Comparison Shop: Another way to save money while shopping online is to compare prices on multiple websites. With a few clicks, you can easily compare prices on different websites to ensure you're getting the best deal.

3. Shop During Sales: Many online retailers offer sales and special promotions throughout the year, so keep an eye out for those. Some websites even have a dedicated section for clearance items, where you can find great deals on products that are being phased out.

4. Use Cashback Sites: Cashback sites offer customers a percentage of their purchase price back in the form of cashback. When you shop through a cashback site, you'll earn a certain percentage back

on your purchase, which can be redeemed for cash or as a credit towards future purchases.

5. Take Advantage of Free Shipping: Shipping costs can add up quickly, especially when shopping for multiple items. To save money, look for retailers that offer free shipping, or sign up for a free trial of a shipping program like Amazon Prime. Some retailers also offer free shipping for orders over a certain amount, so consider consolidating your purchases to take advantage of this offer.

6. Use Price Tracking Tools: Price tracking tools allow you to track the price of a specific item over time and notify you when the price drops. This is especially useful for big-ticket items or for those who have a set budget for a specific item.

7. Look for Refurbished or Used Items: Shopping for refurbished or used items can be a great way to save money while shopping online. You can often find great deals on gently used items, and refurbished items are often just as good as new, but at a lower price.

Shopping online can be a great way to save money, especially if you take advantage of the various money-saving tips mentioned above. By using coupon codes, comparison shopping, shopping during sales, using cashback sites, taking advantage of free shipping, using price tracking tools, and looking for refurbished or used items, you can enjoy the convenience of online shopping while also saving money.

Saving money on hobbies: How to enjoy your hobbies without spending too much

Hobbies are a great way to spend your leisure time, but they can also add up quickly. From buying new equipment to paying for classes or events, hobbies can quickly drain your bank account. However, with a little creativity and planning, you can still enjoy your hobbies without breaking the bank. Here are some tips for saving money on your hobbies:

Prioritize your hobbies:

Start by considering which hobbies you enjoy the most and which ones you can do without. By focusing on the hobbies you love the most, you can save money by avoiding the ones you don't enjoy as much.

Get creative:

Think about alternative ways to engage in your hobbies. For example, if you love photography, instead of buying a new camera, try using your smartphone camera or borrow a camera from a friend. You can also try practicing your photography skills in your local park instead of paying for a trip to a scenic location.

Look for free or low-cost options:

Many cities offer free or low-cost classes, workshops, and events for a variety of hobbies. Check your local community center or library for information on classes or events in your area.

Buy used or refurbished equipment:

If you need to buy equipment for your hobby, look for used or refurbished options. Sites like eBay, Craigslist, and Facebook Marketplace offer used items at a fraction of the cost of new equipment.

Join a club or group:

Joining a club or group centered around your hobby can be a great way to save money. By sharing resources, such as tools and supplies, you can save money on the costs of your hobby.

Trade skills:

Consider trading skills with others who have complementary hobbies. For example, if you're into gardening, trade skills with someone who is into woodworking. This way, you can save money on equipment and supplies by sharing resources.

Plan ahead:

Planning ahead can help you save money on your hobbies. By setting a budget, you can avoid overspending on equipment and supplies. Planning ahead can also help you find deals and promotions on the items you need for your hobby.

By following these tips, you can continue to enjoy your hobbies without putting too much strain on your budget. With a little creativity and planning, you can save money and still have fun with your hobbies.

Money-saving apps: How to use technology to save money

Technology has revolutionized many aspects of our lives, including our finances. With so many money-saving apps available, it's easier than ever to take control of your spending and start saving money. In this chapter, we will explore some of the most popular money-saving apps and how you can use them to reach your financial goals.

1. Budgeting apps

Budgeting apps are designed to help you track your spending and create a budget that works for you. Those apps link to your bank accounts and credit cards, automatically categorizing your spending and providing you with a clear picture of your income and expenses. With this information, you can create a budget that allows you to save more money and reduce your spending in areas where you may be overspending.

2. Cashback and rewards apps

Cashback and rewards apps offer you the opportunity to earn money back on your purchases by shopping through their app. Those apps also offer special deals and promotions, making it even easier to save money on your purchases.

3. Coupon apps

Coupon apps allow you to save money by finding discounts and promotions on your favorite products and services. Simply search for the product or service you're interested in, and the app will provide you with a list of available coupons and promo codes. This can be a great way to save money on everyday purchases like groceries, clothing, and entertainment.

4. Investment apps

Investment apps allow you to invest small amounts of money in a variety of stocks, bonds, and other investment options. Those apps offer educational resources and tools to help you make informed investment decisions, so you can grow your wealth over time.

5. Money transfer apps

Money transfer apps allow you to quickly and easily send money to friends and family. Apps like Venmo, PayPal, and Cash App make it easy to send money, and some even offer instant transfers. This can be a convenient and cost-effective way to send money, especially if you need to send money quickly.

There are many money-saving apps available to help you reach your financial goals. Whether you're looking to create a budget, earn cashback on your purchases, find discounts, invest your money, or send money to friends and family, there's an app for that. By incorporating these apps into your financial routine, you can take control of your spending and start saving money today.

Staying Committed to Frugality: How to Maintain Your Frugal Lifestyle Over Time

Adopting a frugal lifestyle can be a challenge, especially if you're used to spending money freely. However, the benefits of living frugally - saving money, reducing debt, and increasing financial security - make the effort worth it. In this chapter, we'll explore some tips for staying committed to a frugal lifestyle and avoiding common pitfalls.

Set goals and track progress:

Setting clear financial goals is a key part of maintaining a frugal lifestyle. Write down your goals, whether it's paying off debt, saving for a down payment on a house, or simply building up your emergency fund. Keeping track of your progress is also important. For example, you could create a budget spreadsheet, keep a spending diary, or use a budgeting app to monitor your spending and savings.

Stay organized:

Organizing your finances is a crucial part of maintaining a frugal lifestyle. Keep track of your bills and due dates, create a budget and stick to it, and use technology to help you save money and avoid overspending. Apps can help you stay organized and on track.

Avoid impulse purchases:

Impulse purchases can be a big drain on your finances, especially if you're trying to maintain a frugal lifestyle. To avoid impulse purchases, try to stick to a shopping list, avoid browsing the mall or online shopping sites when you're bored or stressed, and consider a 24-hour waiting period before making any big purchases.

Use coupons and sales:

Using coupons and taking advantage of sales can help you save money on groceries, clothing, and other everyday expenses. You can find coupons in your local newspaper, online, or through shopping apps. When shopping online, take the time to compare prices and look for discounts or promo codes.

Shop secondhand:

Shopping secondhand can be a great way to save money and reduce waste. Consider shopping at thrift stores, garage sales, and online marketplaces like eBay and Facebook Marketplace for gently used clothing, furniture, and household items.

Re-evaluate your expenses regularly:

It's important to regularly re-evaluate your expenses to see if you're spending too much money in any one area. For example, if you're spending a lot of money on eating out, consider cooking more meals at home, or if you're spending a lot on entertainment, consider finding free or low-cost alternatives.

Stay motivated:

Staying motivated can be a challenge, especially when you're making big changes to your spending habits.

Surround yourself with supportive friends and family, reward yourself when you reach your financial goals, and don't be too hard on yourself if you slip up. Remember that frugality is a journey, not a destination, and that small changes can add up to big savings over time.

Find frugal alternatives to your favorite activities:

Living frugally doesn't mean giving up all the things you love. Instead, find frugal alternatives to your favorite activities, such as hiking instead of going to the movies, or hosting potluck dinners instead of eating out.

Living frugally takes effort, but the rewards - both financial and personal - make it worth it. By setting goals, staying organized, avoiding impulse purchases, shopping secondhand, re-evaluating your expenses, staying motivated, and finding frugal alternatives, you can maintain a frugal lifestyle and achieve financial security over time.

Conclusion

In conclusion, frugality is a mindset that involves making conscious and deliberate choices with your money, in order to save and make the most of your resources. It's about being mindful of your spending, cutting back on expenses where you can, and maximizing your earning potential. There are countless ways to adopt a frugal lifestyle, from reducing your grocery bill to cutting cable, from freelancing to growing your own food. By taking small steps in the right direction, you can improve your financial situation, save money for the future, and live a more fulfilling life.

But the key to making a frugal lifestyle stick is staying committed over time. This means being disciplined in your spending, making a plan and sticking to it, and seeking out new ways to save and improve your financial situation. It can also mean having a support system in place, whether it's friends or family members who share your frugal values, or online communities where you can connect with others and exchange tips and advice.

Ultimately, the journey to becoming more frugal is a personal one, and it will look different for everyone. But by adopting this mindset and making small changes in your spending habits, you can improve your financial situation, increase your savings, and find greater peace of mind and security. So go ahead, take control of your finances, and start living the frugal life today.

Thank you for taking the time to read this book. I hope that it has provided valuable insights and practical tips on how to save money and improve your financial situation. Your feedback is important to me, and I would be grateful if you could leave a positive review on Amazon. Your review will not only help others make an informed decision about the book but also encourage me to continue creating helpful resources for you. Thank you again for your support.

Printed in Great Britain
by Amazon

42581959R00036